To The Tobins,

Wishing you the
Best in Life!

God Bless,

James E. Small III

Life, Love, and Beyond

Life, Love, and Beyond

The Poetic Storybook

James E. Small III

VANTAGE PRESS
New York

FIRST EDITION

All rights reserved, including the right of
reproduction in whole or in part in any form.

Copyright © 1992 by James E. Small III

Published by Vantage Press, Inc.
516 West 34th Street, New York, New York 10001

Manufactured in the United States of America
ISBN: 0-533-10187-5

0 9 8 7 6 5 4 3 2 1

To the loving memory of my grandmother, Annie Mae Small. I miss you, Grandma.

Special Thanks to . . .
God, my mother and father (Cassandra and Jim), Reenee, Tink, and Lynn.

Contents

Preface ix

1. Friends 1
2. Love 4
3. Faith 16
4. Family 23
5. Humanity 27

Preface

This book is for everyone. It is for any and every person who enjoys the beauty of reading. The purpose of this book is to provide an entertaining and thought-stimulating journey through some of the various stages of life. This book is not simply intended to be a book of poetry only for people who enjoy poems, but rather a poetic storybook for all people who enjoy reading.

Life, Love, and Beyond

Chapter 1
Friends

Friends. What would the world be like if we didn't have friends? They are a very special group of people. They come in all shapes and sizes, colors, and forms. Friends are the ones we call and talk to on the phone for hours. They are the ones we go places with. They share in our happiness and comfort us in our grief.

Yes, the world is a lot more enjoyable place because of the people we call friends. You know how it makes you feel when you have a good friend. It makes you want to say . . .

> Friends are a dime-a-dozen
> and very few are true,
> but I really did get lucky
> when I first met you.

You really are lucky when you have a true friend. True friends are a rare breed, but there are definitely plenty of those "other" types of friends, the type of person who is only your friend when it is convenient for him. It makes you wonder after a while if the person really is a . . . Friend of Mine . . .

> You said you were a friend of mine
> and asked me for a loan,
> but when it was time to pay me back

all you did was moan.
You said you were a friend of mine
and asked to use my car,
but when it was time to get it back,
it resembled a battle scar.
You said you were a friend of mine
and that you wanted to meet my girl,
but when I saw my lady next,
you'd promised her the world.
You said you were a friend of mine
and is this how all your friends you do?
Don't count me on that list again
because, as of now, we're through!

It can leave a bad taste in your mouth when you realize that someone who you thought was a friend was really no friend at all. Unfortunately, we do come in contact with people who are only friends in name but not deed. When we go through experiences with "false" friends, it should only strengthen the value of yet another type of friend. This type of friend is the kind who has been your friend for as long as you can remember. This friend is a Timeless Friend . . .

I hadn't seen you in a while,
but we were childhood best friends.
Then life's travel took us separate ways
and our friendship seemed to end.
It felt like we were always together
for every hour of the day.
Then we grew a little older
and we went a different way.
You were no longer by my side
and for a long time we didn't talk.
You were no longer right around the corner,

        indeed, much farther than a short walk.
        Now once again our paths have crossed
        and it feels like we were never apart.
    I guess the truly close friendships stay forever
        and are forever in our heart.

It feels good. It feels extremely good inside to know that the person you were once so close to is still someone you feel close to. True friendships are rare and false friendships are a dime a dozen. They come cheaply. Old friendships can stand the test of time, and pure friendships are, regardless of the situation, strong.

        I would have said, "I told you so,"
        but it didn't seem like the time.
        I could see the pain that you were in
        and your pain felt like mine.
        I could have said, "I told you so,"
        but you had to learn for yourself.
        Now the knowledge that you possess
        is worth a world of wealth.
        I could have said, "I told you so,"
        and repeated it till no end,
        but I won't say, "I told you so."
        Instead I say, "I'm still your friend."

That's what friends are for. They are there to share in the happiness and to comfort when there's grief. On those other times, they are there to share in our lives. Friends. What would the world be like without them?

Chapter 2

Love

Love. Love has been called and probably is the ultimate emotion. It is the ultimate experience. Love is ubiquitous and its power goes far beyond the realm of friendship.

Think of the emotional tidal wave that is caused by love. When you're in love and the tide is high, love is the greatest feeling, the highest high, and the utmost experience. When you're riding the wave of love, you overflow with confidence and stay seemingly filled with energy. The thrills, the passion, and the desire will never be greater than the ones you experience while you are in love. Love is both inspirational and motivational.

Indeed, love is among life's greatest pleasures. There is no real way to define it, because of the individuality it takes on for different people. If someone was to ask you, after a long pause, you might say something like, love is . . .

To love . . .
To love is . . .
That unexplainable feeling.
To love is . . .
A lesson in life everyone must gain.
To love is . . .
To share in emotions.
To love is . . .
To experience the joy and the pain.

If love is a pleasure, a young love must be an overwhelming sensation. We've all had that "first love" or "puppy love." It was our first chance to test the waters and ride that tidal wave called love. Can you remember when it happened? If so, can you remember how it felt?

Young Love

It doesn't come very often,
but you'll know it from the start.
You can tell by your nervousness
and the pitter-patter of your heart.
You'll think of many thoughts,
but they'll all be of one kind.
The vision of that new person
will stay embedded in your mind.
So much more will follow
in this new relationship sent from above.
You'll learn a lot about living
when you experience a young love.

Yes, that young love is something I'm sure will never be forgotten. All of those classes filled with daydreaming. All those nights you tried to imagine what you would say the next time you saw your young love. Out of all those thoughts and emotions, how would you ever figure out what to say?

Thoughts of a Young Love

I searched and searched
for some words to say,
the way you make me feel
all through the night and all through the day.
I looked in the deepest, darkest,
and all the corners of my mind,
but as I expected,
words so beautiful are hard to find.
I really did know it,
right from the start,
with your charm and wit,
you stole away my heart.
In the future if I don't say very much,
of course you'll know the reason why.
Just look at the warmth in my smile
and the sparkle in my eye.
Hopefully, if everything
turns out right,
I'll see you real soon,
I'll see you tonight.

Young love is so wonderful and innocent that our society has designated specific special events for the promotion of young love. You know the events I'm talking about, the school dances and the proms. If you were one of the lucky ones, you had already found your young love and you knew who would accompany you to the big dance. However, there were those who were less fortunate. They were the people still searching for their young love.

Oh, they did go to the dance, but they went alone. Their night was spent in search of . . .

When the music had first started,
I glanced across the room.
There were many in attendance,
but only one who made my heart go boom.
She stood there in sheer elegance,
the epitome of style and grace.
She had a lovely figure
to complement her darling face.
As the D.J. spun the records,
I slowly took my time,
trying to select the proper words
from the ones jumbled in my mind.
My footsteps were deliberate and firm,
her beauty had me locked into a trance.
That's when I uttered the timeless phrase,
"Excuse me, can we dance?"

Young love is definitely a wonderful and adventurous time in our lives. However, that tidal wave known as love keeps on rolling. It rolls us right on into new stages of our lives and relationships. The newness of young love is now gone and a different intensity level now sets in. This new intensity level now carries with it factors of monumental significance, trust and respect. Trust and respect now become lifelines to the maintenance of your love. It is definitely a Matter of Trust . . .

I can't watch you every day of the week
or keep an eye on you in my sleep.
I won't be around every place that you go
and some of the people you deal with I won't know.
Your other friends and activities are your personal taste;
it's not my job to try to investigate the case.
There are many things you could do when we're apart,

but that absence is no reason to question you in my heart.
When we are together there's a special magic for me,
but standing side by side we can't always be.
While we share life's journey there is a definite must,
no matter the place, for us to endure, it's simply a matter of trust.

Trust is by no means an easy thing to do, especially when you are talking about your heart.

The power of love is not limited to its high points. That is another reason love is known as the ultimate emotion. Just like the ocean, the tidal wave of love is not always calm and at peace. When the waves of love get rocky, they can rip and tear you apart inside. They can make you sad and take you to your worst moments and your lowest low. Love can make you sick to your stomach and fill you with jealousy and anguish. Yes, the tidal wave of love just keeps on rolling from the high points, the low points, and every conceivable point in-between.

Confusion

It's not my fault
It's not your fault
It's no one's fault at all.
I'm not to blame
You're not to blame
It's just a dirty shame.
I don't know why
You don't know why
But we both have reason to pout.
I'm not sure how I feel

> You're not sure how you feel
> Neither of us knows what's really real.
> What do we say
> What do we do
> Love can be so confusing.

When trust and respect have been established, clear and open communication must be maintained. Trust and respect seem to develop over a period of time. Communication, on the other hand, must be continually worked at. Good communication is not easy. People often hear what is said to them, but they don't always listen. The same exact words can also mean two totally different things to two different people. These lapses in good communication can be straining on a love relationship.

> It wasn't supposed to be this way;
> it was supposed to be a relaxed evening
> at the end of a long day.
> Everything was to be so right, so good,
> but the whole scenario changed
> when some words were misunderstood.
> Then it became a battle of might,
> two tremendous opposing forces,
> each determined to prove they were right.
> There was pride at stake, honor to be won,
> neither side willing to admit they could be wrong
> once the argument had begun.
> It all started from something very small;
> it was a minor trivial issue
> that should have been nothing at all.

Then tempers flared and voices rose amid continuous chatter—think about it, who's right or who's wrong. If you really care for each other, does it really matter?

Trust, respect, and good communication are just a few of the ingredients in the tidal wave known as love. A proper blend of those ingredients can have you riding high on the waves of love. If an imbalance of those ingredients occurs, the ride could get rocky. The nonexistence of any of those ingredients and you're almost guaranteed to be washed under by the tidal wave.

Wouldn't it be so much easier if when we fell in love we knew it would be a sure thing? On second thought, is anything in life a sure thing?

Life is a gamble,
a chance that we all must take.
Do we pick the longshot or the favorite?
Do we win or do we break?
Life is a gamble.
Do we bet some or do we bet all?
It's a tough choice to decide,
it could mean the big jump or the big fall.
Life is a gamble.
When do we bet and what do we bet on?
If we bet too soon, the odds change.
If we wait too late, the chance is gone.
Life is a gamble.
To bet all on a longshot could be a great gain,
but the high risk of losing
could mean severe pain.
Life is a gamble.
To bet little on a favorite sounds like a good bet,
but the Hands of Fate could turn
and we could be losers yet.
Life is a gamble.
We must bet based upon how we feel.
We must look at the odds, analyze our chances,

and with ourselves be real.
Like is a gamble.
And with myself I'm going to be true.
I've weighed the odds and looked at my chances
and I'm betting it all, on you.

Love is a gamble. It is a gamble that carries the potential for heartache and disappointment. It is a risk we must take and a decision we must make entirely on our own. No one else can tell us how we feel or what we think when we're in love. It's an entirely different thought process; single becomes duo, me becomes us, and one becomes two. Life becomes . . . the Power of Two . . .

In this life we live
there's a lot that must be done,
and the burden can be quite heavy
when it's carried just by one.
There are some things some people can't do
and some things that others can.
There's a difference in every woman
and a unique aspect to every man.
If you have a weakness that is my strength,
you can grow stronger through me.
If I have a weakness that is your strength,
together stronger, we both will be.
As long as you live, you'll never be alone.
I'll always fully support you.
No matter the burden, all we need to do
is use the Power of Two!

Isn't it wonderful! Isn't it great! Isn't it just terrific when you take that chance on love and get it right! It makes you feel on top of the world. When you have that love power working inside, you feel like Superman or Wonder Woman. It's so good . . . you feel . . .

> I feel sunshine all through me
> even on a rainy day.
> I feel good all over
> ever since you came my way.
> My energy level pulsates,
> there is definite pep in my stride.
> Your love is my motivation
> that fills my heart with pride.
> When in a crowd of people,
> I feel the urge to sing,
> "She is my Queen,"
> and I to her am King.
> I've made the ultimate commitment
> to be forever by your side.
> I'll always be there for you
> as a friend, a lover, and a guide.

When you've found love and it's working out the way you always hoped it would, there's no better feeling in the world. The people with that type of love are the lucky ones.

Everybody isn't always that lucky. There are still some people who are looking for love. They are looking and hoping and searching to find that one person to come into their lives and share their life and their love.

> My love for you is constant
> and I couldn't love you more.
> My heart awaits your arrival
> just like an open door.
> That door wants you to come in,
> get comfortable and take a seat.

> You are the one last piece to the puzzle
> that would make my life complete.
> The door will remain open
> for only you to see.
> My heart awaits your arrival
> to share my life with me.

It can be tough when you're looking for love, but even tougher once you've lost it.

> This morning when I woke up
> as I calmly lay in place,
> I looked toward the bright shining sun,
> but all I saw was your face.
> You had left me some time ago,
> gone with hardly a trace,
> but this afternoon as I looked at the waiter,
> all I saw was your face.
> I had said that we couldn't stay together
> and that's when I fell from your grace,
> but tonight as I looked into my plate at dinner,
> all I saw was your face.
> Now I realize what would truly make me happy
> and I wouldn't care what happened to the rest of the
> human race,
> if only you were always with me
> and all I saw was your face.

If finding love is one of the best feelings in the world, then losing love is definitely one of the worst.

> I'm thinking about you now
> and wondering if you're home.
> Then a frightening thought passes,

that you are not alone.
I think of you quite often
really much more than I should.
If I could sometimes do so,
I'd stop those thoughts if I could.
Then thoughts of you overcome me
and at the first phone I see I leap.
Then after I impatiently dial your number,
I hear you say, "Wait for the beep."
In my mind we are together,
in reality we're apart,
but those constant lovely thoughts of you
keep you in my heart.

Sometimes when you think back on the love you've lost, you probably said and did some things that you didn't really mean. When emotions run high, we often say things before we think about what we're saying. It is also true that sometimes we don't say everything that we should.

Did I ever say, "I'm sorry"
for all the pain I caused?
I know it doesn't heal the wound
like a bandage or some gauze.
I was a very selfish person,
all caught up in what I wanted to do.
I didn't fully realize
what my actions meant to you.
I am truly, deeply sorry
and if I didn't say it then,
I want you to know I really mean it
and would like to make amends.

Love. It is probably the ultimate emotion. Whether it is young love or old love, new love or lost love or any other kind of love, the emotions will never be greater than when love is involved.

Love is the highest high and the lowest low. It can be thrills and passion and desire or agony, distress and pain. Love is the ultimate experience. "... and the greatest of these is love" (1 Corinthians 13:13, *The Way, the Living Bible* (Wheaton, IL: Tyndale House, 1971).

Chapter 3
Faith

Faith. Faith is the power of believing. The truly amazing thing about the power of faith is that it usually is a belief in something that cannot be proved. Belief in God or religion or any number of spiritual things can be known as faith. Isn't it wonderful when we can believe in something that cannot be proven? Isn't it beautiful when we have faith?

> You've got to believe
> if you want your dreams to come true
> that there is a higher power
> than the one in me and you.
> You've got to believe
> with all your heart and soul
> that having faith in your life
> is worth more than pot of gold.
> You've got to believe!

Yes, in today's worrisome, troublesome society, faith is a necessity. There is instability in the economy. There is drug usage seemingly out of control. Transmittable diseases now have no cure. The extended family no longer exists. The divorce rate is nearly 50 percent. In many cases the basic family unit has only one parent at home. Without faith our world can feel like a very cold and lonely place. Faith is the one thing that lets us know that we have not been abandoned, we are not alone . . .

> I never walk alone
> no matter where I go.
> I have a silent partner
> that you may or may not know.
> I never play alone
> regardless of the game.
> I have a silent partner
> who has a special name.
> I never work alone
> in any type work place.
> I have a silent partner
> who never leaves a trace.
> I never do anything alone
> no matter where I trod.
> I have a silent partner,
> it's the ubiquitous power of God.

Having faith is a very comfortable feeling. It relieves the loneliness and assists with the stress. Faith does for you what you can't do for yourself.

> It's out of my hands now,
> the burden was more than I could stand.
> The pressure was too much for my shoulders
> and the weight too great for my hands.
> I don't worry anymore,
> I took those problems off my chest;
> I shipped them off in prayer
> to the one who handles problems best.
> I feel much better now,
> I lifted that stress up off of me,

> I took everything to God in prayer
> and in return, He set my spirit free.

Drugs and disease can really stress us out, but it is that matter of the heart that tears us apart inside. That's right: love. We already discussed the power of love and its tidal-wave effects, but faith can help us in dealing with our love situations too.

> I can't love you any better
> any more than I already do.
> Ask the Lord up above,
> I love you, for you.
> I've said it over and over,
> I've told you time and time again,
> if you don't know by now,
> I just don't know when.
> I'm not going to keep saying it,
> but I do know what I'll do.
> I'll ask the Lord to give me strength
> to keep on loving you.

Life and love offer us daily challenges. Faith offers us a way to meet those challenges. It's not always easy, but we only get one life and we have to learn how to enjoy it.

> You have to learn to love life
> and all it has to give.
> You have to thank the Lord above
> for the privilege it is to live.
> You have to learn to love life
> and not just on a good day.
> You have to count your blessings too
> when things don't go your way.

You have to learn to love life
when it seems you're all alone.
Your prayers will soon be answered
and soon you'll find a home.
You have to learn to love life,
but first you must believe.
It is with the power from above
that allows you to achieve.
You have to learn to love life,
so much happier you will be
when you put your faith in the Lord
from now till eternity.

There are many things that faith gives us, such as comfort and strength. There is also another thing that faith gives us whose value can never be underestimated. That other thing is . . . a second chance . . .

Second chances.
What are they
and when do they come?
Second chances.
Do we get them
or do we only get one?
Second chances.
Do they exist?
If so, what are they for?
Second chances.
Did we do it all the first time
or is there room for one chance more?
Second chances.
Does everybody get them
or is it some unspoken rule?
Second chances.

Yes, they do exist,
They're an opportunity to change the wrongs to right.
Second chances
are a new beginning
Like the changing to day from night.
Second chances
come only at special times,
only when they are deserved, only when earned.
Second chances
are a measure of a person,
of how much we now know and how much we've learned.
Second chances.
When we get one,
we must recognize what's been unfurled.
Second chances.
Thank the Lord we have them.
They are a Supreme Gift to the world.

When your faith is strong, you usually do get a second chance. When that second chance comes, you should be thankful for the opportunity. It is when we receive that second chance at something in life or at life itself that we should voice our appreciation while we still can.

Before I die
let me make some things perfectly clear,
some things that need to be said
and some things that a few need to hear.
First of all, I want to thank God
for taking and leading me by the hand,
for guiding me through this life
from birth, through adolescence, to a man.
Then let me thank my family,
all of my relatives and especially Mom and Dad,

> those who stood by and supported me
> during the best of times and also when things went bad.
> Before I die
> let me acknowledge the ones who are my friends,
> those special relationships that I cherish
> and that I hope will endure till the end.
> Let me thank the love that I lost.
> We were together and now we're apart,
> but you added so much goodness to my life
> that you'll always own a piece of my heart.
> Let me shout the praises
> of the love that I found,
> the one that put all the pieces in place,
> the one that makes my whole world go round.
> And I say this
> to all the people of the world,
> have concern for one another and love the children,
> each boy and every girl.

I don't know when this life is going to end, the month, the year, the how or even the why, but remember the things I've said (that's why I'm saying them). Before I die.

Faith. Faith is the belief in God or religion or any number of spiritual things. It does not really matter what God you believe in, what religion you practice or what spiritual things you praise.

There are many various religions and each is significant. Everyone does not practice the same religion or worship the same God, but we should respect each other and acknowledge the fact that we are the same in our belief, that there is a greater power, whatever or whoever we believe that power to be.

What does really matter is that we realize and believe that there is a power far greater than the one in you and me. That greater power can and does help us deal with the ups and downs, stress and strife, that this life has to offer. That greater power is often what sustains us and carries us as we strive to make it from day to day. That greater power is called faith. You've got to believe!

Chapter 4
Family

Family. Mother, father, son, daughter, sister, brother, aunt, uncle, cousin, in-law, grandmother, and grandfather are all people who are members of our family. The family is the basic unit of society. It is the origin from which we grow. It is the foundation for what we know and learn.

There will be many people who come into our lives, but no one will be there before Mom and Dad. They are the two people who give us our start in the world. Dad has to wait several months before he can meet his newborn child, but Mom, she knows her child much sooner than that. She is our channel into this world and is and always will be the first lady in our lives.

She is quite a lovely lady
and the strength of the family.
I come from her flesh
and her blood is in me.
She is a very intelligent woman
and many lessons she has taught.
My understanding is so much greater
because her lessons were not for naught.
She is a very respected person
who talks with dignity.
My morals are so much higher

>   because of standards she set for me.
>   She is a very caring person
>   who helps her fellow man.
>   I've learned the importance of good will
>   and offer it when I can.
>   She is a very religious woman
>   who taught me how to pray.
>   It is the message in those prayers
>   that carries me from day to day.
>   She is an extraordinary lady
>   filled with the virtues of no other.
>   Her importance in my life is unparalleled
>   because she is my mother.

Mom is quite a lady, but Dad is quite a guy too. When we deal with Mom, we tend to be more emotional and sensitive all the time. When we deal with Dad, we might only get emotional and sensitive once a year . . .

>   It's that time again
>   when "Father's Day" comes around
>   to tell you, Dad, "Thank you,"
>   because you never let me down.
>   You were there right from the start
>   and I know you'll be there until the end.
>   That's why you're not just my father,
>   you're also my best friend.

The family is definitely the origin and base of society, and the mother and father are the base of the family.

However, here is also another type of relative in the family. That relative is the one who has gone beyond life as we know it.

You brightened our days
with your garden and flowers.
You blessed us with your presence
for many days and many hours.
But as we all must do
you left us one day,
but thank you very much,
we enjoyed your stay.
Now your spirit, with His will fly.

The loss of a family member is a very difficult and traumatic time. It is a time when families come together, to not only mourn their loss, but also to draw strength and comfort from each other. Time will move on after a death in the family has occurred, but the memory and spirit of that loved one, perhaps a grandmother or grandfather, will continue to live on . . .

It has been a few years now
and your spirit lives on.
You may not be here with us,
but your presence is far from gone.
You're a continued source of inspiration,
someone to whom we can pray.
Your motherly touch and heavenly grace
help us make it through each passing day.
No, we have not forgotten you,
we think of you from dusk till dawn.
Because of how wonderful you were,
your spirit lives on.

No matter how much time passes, the memory still lives on . . .

The time has passed so quickly
and the years have moved along,
to think it has now been ages
since we had to say so-long.
Many years ago
that's when you did depart,
but your love and motherly influence
remain embedded in our hearts.
To say we no longer think of you
would surely be a lie
because of the beautiful way you lived your life,
you are a continued example for us to live by.
We pray to you in the morning
and we pray to you in the night
because we know you're at the right hand of God
making sure your family is all right.
We didn't want you to leave us,
but we understand you had to go.
We still love you very much
and that's what we wanted you to know.

Family. It is where we get our start in this life. Our primary care comes from our parents. Mom and Dad are the foundation of the family from which we grow and learn. They teach us strength and character and provide support. The other relatives in our family also have an effect on our lives and who we are or will become. Each and every person in our family is an essential part of our lives.

Mother, father, son, daughter, sister, brother, aunt, uncle, cousin, in-law, grandmother, grandfather, and those other very special relatives who continue to be a source of inspiration, the ones who have gone Beyond. All are a wonderful part of the basic unit of society, the family.

Chapter 5
Humanity

Humanity. The human race is certainly a diverse group of people. It consists of all shapes and sizes, colors and forms. It consists of relatives, friends, people we fall in love with, and people we hardly know. The human race also teaches us about things, such as death, knowledge and ignorance, disappointment, determination, triumph, and much much more.

Some of us learn about death at an early age. Perhaps, it was a relative or friend. It is also quite possible that the "grown-ups" had some difficulty in explaining just exactly what had happened.

> They said you were coming back.
> They said you'd be back again,
> but the years have kept on coming,
> I thought you were my friend.
> They said you went up above,
> you had gone to the pearly gate,
> but who would want to keep us apart?
> Is that what they call fate?
> We used to have such fun together,
> we played and shared our toys,
> but why did they separate us
> since we were both just little boys?
> I've grown bigger and older now

and I don't know what to do.
It doesn't look like you're coming back,
but I still think of you.

When you first experience death, it's a hard lesson to learn. However, you soon discover that the human race has a lot more lessons to teach.

It used to be so easy,
it used to be such a joy.
My responsibilities were so limited
when I was just a boy.
It used to be a lot of fun,
it used to be playing and laughter all the while.
Life's demands were not yet that great
when I was just a child.
Then someone turned the hands of time
and now I do the best I can;
it's not the way it used to be
now that I'm a man.

Yes, we definitely live and learn. We gain various experience and encounter various types of people. Sometimes certain situations still leave us asking questions. Questions like . . .

Is that the way it was meant to be?
Ten-year-olds talking of sex,
Twelve-year-olds having sex,
Fifteen-year-olds having babies,
Motherhood before high-school graduation,
Is that the way it was meant to be?
First boyfriend in ninth grade?
Engaged in tenth grade,

Housewife and mother in eleventh grade,
High school drop-out,
Is that the way it was meant to be?
No knowledge of the I.U.D.,
Scared of the pill,
Improper use of the condom,
Unwanted pregnancy,
Is that the way it was meant to be?
Sex for fun,
Sex for play,
Sex on every third day,
An abortion,
Is that the way it was meant to be?
With all of our institutions for higher learning,
With all of our knowledge of sexual behavior,
With all of our many forms of contraception,
Teenage mothers, high school dropouts, unwanted pregnancies,
Unnecessary abortions,
Is that the way it was meant to be?

Despite the ignorance that still exists in the human race in dealing with certain issues, there is yet another group of people. This group of individuals is smart and determined. They are the ones who've worked hard, gotten an education, and now ask for one thing from mankind: a chance.

Young, eager, and talented,
he now had his degree.
He was determined to make an impact
and the world would better be.
Filled with bright ideas and spirit,
his college days were done.
Big business needed a new leader

and he vowed to be the one.
He charged to every interview
with resumés in his case.
He was confident in his ability
and wore a smile upon his face.
Then he got what he needed,
it wasn't mystical, magical or free.
He needed a chance to prove himself
and what he got was an opportunity.

There is triumph when we are given the opportunity to prove ourselves, and there can be disappointment when people don't do the things that they say they will.

You said you would like to help me
and you offered me a hand.
You said you would do many things
to help this struggling man.
I was slowly moving forward
and for your help I did not ask.
I was persistent and independent
in facing each coming task.
You said you liked what you saw in me
and you'd help me get ahead,
but your words were only promises
and your promises were soon dead.
I had raised my hopes and dreams,
a huge house, a new car, and a boat,
but all that you helped me get
was a big empty promissory note.
I guess I could be angry
and I guess I could be sad.
You did absolutely nothing for me,
but still I don't feel bad.

> You raised my hopes and dreams
> and for the good life I still yearn,
> but I'll get what I get when I get it
> and what I get *I'll* earn.

Humanity. It is simply the fact of being human. It is diverse and specializes in variety. It provides highs and lows, ups and downs, and all that is in between. The people are all colors, all sizes, and all different. There are many lessons to be learned in life; humanity teaches them.

> J.S. I once did an equation and factored in Friends,
> Love, Faith, Family, and Humanity
> And the answer that I came up with was . . .

LIFE, LOVE, AND BEYOND
(The Poetic Storybook)